MW01118078

MAKING A DIFFERENCE: ATHLETES WHO ARE CHANGING THE WORLD

KEVIN DURANT

IN THE COMMUNITY

MATT ANNISS

Britannica®
Educational Publishing

IN ASSOCIATION WITH

ROSEN
EDUCATIONAL SERVICES

Published in 2014 by Britannica Educational Publishing (a trademark of Encyclopædia Britannica, Inc.)
in association with The Rosen Publishing Group, Inc.
29 East 21st Street, New York, NY 10010

Distributed exclusively by Rosen Publishing.
To see additional Britannica Educational Publishing titles, go to rosenpublishing.com

First Edition

Britannica Educational Publishing
J.E. Luebering: Director, Core Reference Group
Anthony L. Green: Editor, Compton's by Britannica

Rosen Publishing
Hope Lourie Killcoyne: Executive Editor
Jeanne Nagle: Senior Editor
Nelson Sá: Art Director

Library of Congress Cataloging-in-Publication Data

Anniss, Matt.
Kevin Durant in the community/Matt Anniss.
        pages cm. — (Making a difference: athletes who are changing the world)
Includes bibliographical references and index.
ISBN 978-1-62275-180-8 (library binding) — ISBN 978-1-62275-183-9 (pbk.) —
ISBN 978-1-62275-184-6 (6-pack)
1. Durant, Kevin, 1998 — Juvenile literature. 2. Basketball players — United States — Biography — Juvenile
literature. 3. African American basketball players — Biography — Juvenile literature. I. Title.
GV884.D868A66 2013
796.323092 — dc23
[B]
                                                                                        2013024589

Manufactured in the United States of America

CONTENTS

An elite athlete and exceptional basketball player, Kevin has never forgotten his humble beginnings and difficult start in life. He works hard to use his fame and wealth to make a difference in the lives of people in need.

In a short space of time, Kevin Durant has become one of the biggest stars in the United States' National Basketball Association (NBA). His appearances at the Olympics have also made him one of the most famous basketball players in the world.

Kevin's story is remarkable. He was raised by his mother in a poor area of Washington, D.C., and from an early age decided to become a professional basketball player. He won a scholarship to attend college in Texas. He stayed for just one year, earning several awards in the process, before being picked up by a professional team in the 2007 NBA Draft.

Since making it in the NBA, Kevin has devoted himself to working with charities that help youngsters from backgrounds similar to his own. The star has now become famous not only for his skills on the basketball court, but also for his contributions to the community.

CHAPTER 1

THE STORY OF KEVIN DURANT

Kevin Durant (born September 29, 1988, in Washington, D.C.) experienced a few bumps along the way to becoming a basketball star. His parents Wanda Durant (later Pratt), an office worker for the federal government, and Wayne Pratt, a police officer at the Library of Congress, separated when Kevin was just eight months old. That left Wanda to raise Kevin and his older brother, Tony Durant, alone.

Although his father came back into his life when Kevin was older, the basketball star spent his early years living with his mom, who often had to work long hours to earn enough money to care for her family.

Even as a child, Kevin displayed the exceptional skills that helped him become a superstar basketball player.

This meant leaving the boys in the care of their grandmother, Barbara Davis.

Wanda wished for her children to grow up understanding the importance of hard work and making the most of their talents. She taught her sons to be approachable and kind to others, and to stay out of trouble.

Being raised by his mom and grandmother had a huge effect on Kevin. Many of his peers drifted into hanging out with the wrong crowd, with no positive focus in their lives. Kevin's mom made sure he focused on other things, especially basketball, at which he excelled.

STAR STATS

In his first and only year at college, Kevin Durant was named 2006–07 Big 12 Player of the Year, the 2007 Naismith College Player of the Year, and the National Association of Basketball Coaches (NABC) Division 1 Player of the Year.

DESTINED FOR STARDOM

From an early age, Kevin fell in love with basketball. His mom was eager for him to play as much as possible, so she helped him join a local Amateur Athletic Union (AAU) youth team. That team, PG Jaguars based in Prince George's County, Maryland, would quickly become one of the best in the country.

When Kevin was 11, his Jaguars team competed in the Youth Basketball of America Tournament. This national championship features AAU youth teams from all over the country. In the 2002 championship game, Kevin's superb performance helped the Jaguars win the tournament.

Afterward, he told his mom that he wanted to play in the NBA. Wanda told Kevin that if he wanted to achieve that dream, he would have to work very hard. So Kevin did. He spent all of his free time working out, practicing, and perfecting his basketball skills. Kevin's hard work and devotion would pay off.

Kevin shooting the ball at the 2006 McDonald's All-American game for the top high school players in North America. By the time he finished high school, Kevin was already marked out as a future NBA great.

COLLEGE SUCCESS

When he finished high school, Kevin was offered a scholarship to attend the University of Texas at Austin. This meant he could attend the university, study, and play for the university's Texas Longhorns basketball team.

Kevin started every one of the University of Texas Longhorns' games in his first year at college. From the outset, he made a huge difference to the team. Kevin was quick on his feet, was a high scorer, and was great at the free-throw line.

STAR STATS

When Kevin left the University of Texas in the summer of 2007, the college decided to retire his jersey, No. 35. No other Longhorns player will wear that number in the future.

The jersey that Kevin wore while playing for the Texas Longhorns is now displayed in a frame as a mark of respect to the awesome player.

In the spring of 2007, the Longhorns finished as runners up in the Big 12 Men's Basketball Tournament. Kevin was named the Most Valuable Player of the tournament after he scored a record 92 points during tournament play. He decided to announce his eligibility for the NBA Draft. This was Kevin's chance to be signed by a professional basketball team, and to make his childhood dream come true.

Immediately after signing with the Seattle Supersonics, Kevin was chosen by Nike to wear and promote their shoes and sportswear.

Star Rookie

The annual NBA Draft gives professional basketball teams the chance to sign the best college players. As one of the country's finest young basketball players, it didn't take Kevin long to find his place with a team. In fact, he was the second player in the whole country to be picked in the 2007 Draft. Kevin was chosen by the Seattle Supersonics, and he signed a multi-million-dollar contract with the basketball team.

Predictably, Kevin immediately made his mark in the NBA. He scored 18 points in his first match for the Sonics, and went on to break a number of team records. At the end of the season, he was named NBA Rookie of the Year, an award given to the most successful first-year professional player.

In 2008, at the end of Kevin's successful first season, it was announced that the Sonics would move from Seattle to Oklahoma, and become the Oklahoma City Thunder. Kevin has remained with the Thunder ever since.

STAR STATS

In his first season with the Sonics, Kevin's points-per-game average of 20.3 broke the Sonics 40-year-old rookie record set by Bob Rule in 1968.

U.S. ALL-STAR

Some basketball players struggle to recapture the form they showed in their rookie season. Kevin Durant is not one of those players. Since making his mark in the 2007–08 season, the basketball star has gone from strength to strength, consistently scoring more points than any other player in the NBA.

At the end of the 2009–10 basketball season, Kevin finished atop the NBA scoring charts. This recognizes players with the best

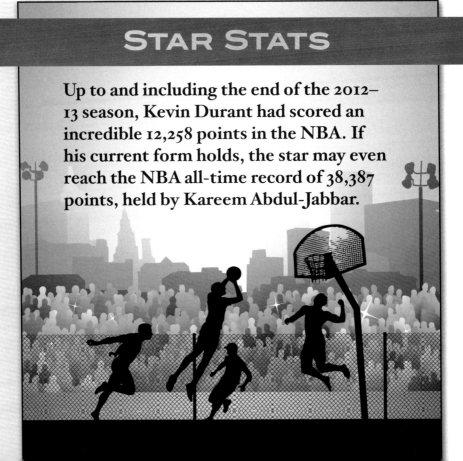

STAR STATS

Up to and including the end of the 2012–13 season, Kevin Durant had scored an incredible 12,258 points in the NBA. If his current form holds, the star may even reach the NBA all-time record of 38,387 points, held by Kareem Abdul-Jabbar.

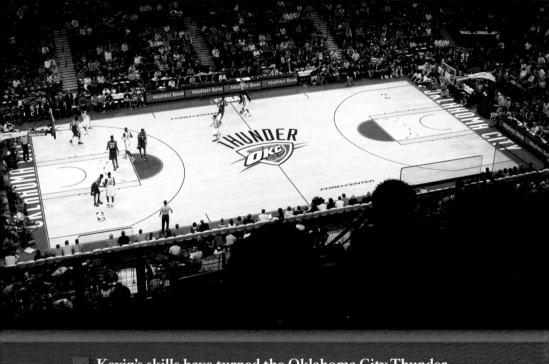

Kevin's skills have turned the Oklahoma City Thunder (here, playing on their home court in Chesapeake Energy Arena) into genuine playoff contenders. This means the team has a chance to become NBA champions.

points-per-game average, figured out by adding up the total number of points scored and dividing that number by the number of games.

In the 2009–10 season, Kevin scored a phenomenal 2,472 points in 82 games, giving him a points-per-game average of 30.1. He topped the charts in the following two years, too, and only narrowly missed out on the award in the 2012–13 season. His high scoring also meant that Kevin has been asked to play in the NBA All-Star Game every year since 2010.

INTERNATIONAL SUPERSTAR

Kevin first started attracting the attention of the U.S. national team's coaches as a student at the University of Texas. In 2007, he was invited to take part in a Team USA training camp, and only narrowly missed out on selection for the 2008 U.S. Olympic basketball team.

Although Kevin is a huge star in the United States, his international performances for Team USA also have made him one of the best-known athletes in the world.

When Kevin did eventually make it onto Team USA, his scoring feats helped the team win the 2010 international FIBA World Championship for the first time since 1994. During the tournament, Kevin broke a number of Team USA records, and was named Most Valuable Player of the tournament.

In 2012, Kevin repeated his performance at the London Olympic Games. Few teams even got close to beating Team USA. The outstanding group of players beat Spain in the final to win the gold medal on the final day of the Games.

STAR STATS

During the course of the 2012 Olympic basketball competition, Kevin scored a total of 156 points, the most points scored by an American in a single Olympic Games.

Here, Kevin (front, far left) poses with Team USA after beating Spain to take the Olympic gold medal at the London Olympic Games in 2012.

A MUCH-LOVED BASKETBALL PLAYER

Kevin Durant's rise to basketball superstar status took only a few years. Just over five years after he left college, Kevin played for Team USA at the London Olympics. During his rise to Olympic champion, Kevin set many scoring records and turned the Oklahoma City Thunder into playoff contenders.

Kevin is an extremely popular player with the public, which is why so many companies have contracted with the star to advertise their products. It is not Kevin's basketball skills alone that make him one of the country's favorite athletes. His easy-going attitude, exemplary behavior, and willingness to help others also contribute to the star's popularity. Since becoming an NBA multimillionaire, Kevin has put some of his fortune toward setting up his own charity, and has said he hopes to inspire young people to better themselves through sport.

STAR STATS

On January 18, 2013, Kevin set a new Oklahoma City Thunder record by scoring 52 points in a single game against the Dallas Mavericks.

CHAPTER 2

SUPPORTING FAMILIES

Kevin Durant seeks to use his success to help others. In doing so, he has become thought of as a community champion. Kevin is well known for his support of charities that work with youngsters who come from disadvantaged backgrounds similar to his own.

In March 2012, Kevin and his mom, Wanda, decided to launch a charity, the Kevin Durant Family Foundation. When Kevin announced that he'd set up the foundation, he singled out his mom for special praise, saying, "My mother taught me to always be strong and always work hard. She's been working hard her whole life for me and my brother. And now, I'm a lot like her in that I work hard for what I want."

True to his word, Kevin worked hard on the charity, setting spending priorities, raising funds, and explaining the foundation's aims. From the outset, the charity's priorities were simple—giving kids opportunities to better themselves, and supporting single parents.

Kevin is determined to foster basketball talent among the next generation. His foundation provides opportunities for kids like these to practice the sport as part of after-school clubs and summer camps.

MAKING FAMILY A PRIORITY

Kevin Durant was inspired to set up his Family Foundation by the role his mom played in his upbringing in Washington, D.C., and the opportunity basketball gave him to escape problems on the city's streets.

The charity's website explains how Kevin came to decide on the foundation's priorities. It states: "When it came time to set the priorities for his foundation... Kevin didn't have to look

STAR STATS

Between 2010 and 2013, Kevin played in four consecutive NBA All-Star games, which feature the best basketball players in the United States. In 2012, Kevin was named All-Star's Most Valuable Player.

Kevin speaks at a 2012 All-Star Weekend press conference. Kevin's foundation supports issues close to his heart, including giving kids a focus to keep them off the streets—just as basketball was his focus.

far. He chose to focus on the very things that have led him to his own success: support from his mom, Wanda Pratt, and the opportunity to engage in neighborhood activities that 'kept him out of trouble.'"

Kevin decided that the charity would concentrate on helping single mothers, giving kids in poor areas a good Christmas, and helping children learn the skills they need to get ahead in life. The charity also supports after-school programs and summer camps.

FUNDING THE FOUNDATION

The Kevin Durant Family Foundation runs some of its own programs, but mostly donates money to other charities. The foundation supports many fundraising initiatives, with the aim of donating money raised to charities that improve the lives of people in need.

Kevin uses some of his vast fortune to pay for various Family Foundation activities, but also raises further money to support the charity's work. The foundation got its start in March 2012 with help from a benefit fundraiser, the Devon Energy KD35 Ball. This event featured dinner, dancing, guest speakers, musical performances, and a charity sale of signed sports memorabilia donated by the NBA All-Star's athlete friends.

Tickets for a seat at the Kevin Durant Family Foundation's KD35 Ball cost around $500. Tickets for one of the best tables in the ballroom cost $25,000. All ticket sales went toward the foundation's charity work.

Basketball jerseys signed by top players were auctioned at the Kevin Durant Family Foundation Ball. Auctioned items included the sportswear worn by Kevin Durant (shown right, playing at the Goodman League in 2011) himself.

CHAPTER 3

MAKING A DIFFERENCE

S ince beginning his NBA career in the fall of 2007, Kevin Durant has proven to be one of basketball's biggest supporters of charities and good causes.

Kevin tries to make as many personal appearances at charity events as he can. He even asks his sponsors, such as Nike, to encourage kids from local youth groups to be involved with his appearances. When Kevin teamed up with Nike to launch a new range of shoes at the House of Hoops in the Harlem neighborhood of New York City in 2012,

Kevin celebrates winning the gold medal in the FIBA World Championships between Team USA and Turkey on September 13, 2010.

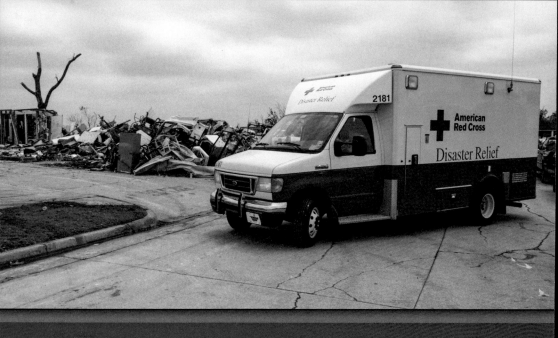

The Kevin Durant Family Foundation pledged $1 million to the American Red Cross to help with the relief effort after the Oklahoma tornado disaster of 2013.

he arranged for teenagers from the city's Polo Grounds Community Center to attend the event.

Kevin is a supporter of a youth music program called P'Tones Records. In 2011, he helped the charity build a recording studio to help teach music to kids in Washington, D.C.

Kevin has also helped in times of crisis. When Oklahoma was devastated by a powerful tornado in May 2013, Kevin used his profile on the social networking site Twitter to encourage his 4.1 million followers to make donations toward the crisis relief fund.

SUPPORTING SINGLE PARENTS

Kevin has never forgotten the sacrifices his hard-working mom made for him during his childhood. Ever since, he has been committed to helping charities that work with single-parent families.

Supporting single-parent families is one of the priorities of the Kevin Durant Family Foundation. Even before setting up the foundation, Kevin was working with charities to support single parents.

In 2011, Kevin organized the biggest all-star charity basketball game that Oklahoma City

STAR STATS

During the 2009–10 season, Kevin set a new Oklahoma City Thunder record for the greatest points-per-game average, an amazing 30.1 points.

has ever seen. Kevin organized the game to raise money for the Oklahoma City Single Parent Support Network. At halftime, fans applauded as Kevin and his mother, Wanda, presented the Oklahoma City Single Parent Support Network with a check for $100,000 to support their vital work in the community.

Almost 13,000 fans crammed into the Cox Convention Center to see Kevin play alongside other top NBA stars, including LeBron James, Chris Paul, Carmelo Anthony, and Michael Beasley.

HELPING KIDS READ

One of the biggest priorities of the Kevin Durant Family Foundation is children's literacy. The reading programs the foundation supports focus on helping children under nine years of age, to ensure literacy at an early age.

One of the charities Kevin has supported most enthusiastically is based at Edwards

Kevin is passionate about early literacy and is aware of the issues that result if it is not encouraged. Experts say that children who cannot read by the end of third grade may fall behind and struggle with literacy as adults.

Elementary in North Oklahoma. The school started a program called Reading Explorers, a series of summer reading camps for youngsters, who spend one day each week reading with teachers, friends, and guest speakers. Kevin has attended reading camps and read to the children.

In 2012, the program began to run after-school reading clubs. This was partly made possible thanks to money from the Kevin Durant Family Foundation.

STAR STATS

Along with scoring on his own, Kevin also sets up scoring opportunities for others. Up to, and including, the end of the 2012–13 season, Kevin had recorded 1,447 scoring assists in his NBA career. That means his passes to teammates led to points for his team.

THE SEASON OF GIVING

In interviews with the press, Kevin has talked about how much the holidays mean to him, Christmas in particular. Kevin's mother worked tirelessly to be able to afford to buy presents for her sons at Christmas, and this has made a great impression on the basketball star. Since 2007, Kevin has tried to make Christmas special for disadvantaged kids.

As a rookie NBA player, in December 2007, Kevin took 26 youngsters on a shopping trip in Seattle, and also took them for dinner afterward. The next year, Kevin handed

STAR STATS

As of the end of the 2012-13 season, Kevin Durant has played 461 regular season games for the Oklahoma City Thunder and the Seattle Supersonics, 54 games in the playoffs, and four NBA All-Star Games.

Along with donating funds, Kevin helps in person at charity events. Here, he helps distribute groceries during the 2013 NBA Cares Day of Service at the Houston Food Bank in Texas.

out coats, gloves, and gifts to 60 children at an after-school program for inner-city kids in Oklahoma City.

Since then, Kevin has continued what he calls the Kevin's Christmas initiative. Every year, the basketball player makes a different contribution to disadvantaged young people. One year, he coordinated a "giving tree" event in Oklahoma City. Youngsters wrote down their wishes for Christmas on paper ornaments, and members of the community tried to make those wishes come true by purchasing the gift listed on each ornament.

In April 2013, Kevin took part in a charity bowling tournament with fellow Oklahoma City Thunder stars Russell Westbrook (center) and Serge Ibaka (right). All funds raised were donated to Westbrook's Why Not? Foundation.

AFTER-SCHOOL CLUB

When asked by a journalist what made him start playing basketball as a child, Kevin replied, "My mom thought it would be a fun activity to keep me away from the streets." Kevin has never forgotten this, and has become a passionate supporter of clubs and activity programs that give kids from similar, inner-city backgrounds a positive focus. The Oklahoma City Thunder star has given generously to organizations that offer youth sports coaching and other after-school programs, including the Maryland Jaguars Youth Organization, the Seat Pleasant Activity Center, and the Community Kinship Coalition.

In March 2013, Durant also helped fellow Thunder player Thabo Sefolosha raise money for after-school sports programs in Mamelodi, South Africa. Kevin attended the star-studded "A Night for Africa" fundraising event and said "It's such a great cause... we're all going to try to help as much as we can." The fundraising night reportedly raised $250,000 for after-school programs for children in South Africa.

STAR STATS

In a game against Utah in April 2010, Kevin Durant scored seven three-point baskets, a career-best scoring feat.

CHAPTER 4

LEADING BY EXAMPLE

Basketball websites feature page after page of articles praising Kevin Durant as a great role model. The way that Kevin trains tirelessly, plays with true passion and determination, and conducts himself when off the basketball court set a great example to young people who follow the star.

Kevin faces the media during a Team USA exhibition game in July 2012. The game is part of the Hoops for Troops program that connects hundreds of military personnel and their families through activities such as basketball games.

After the move to Oklahoma, Kevin became famous for turning up to training 90 minutes early so he could spend more time in the gym lifting weights and practicing his shooting. He'd usually be the last to leave, too, having practiced longer and harder than his teammates.

Another example of Kevin's character can be found in the story behind the number "35" on his basketball jersey. Thirty-five was the age of Kevin's first basketball coach, Charles "Chucky" Craig, when he was shot dead in Washington, D.C. As a mark of respect toward the coach who helped shape his early basketball career, Kevin wears No. 35.

STAR STATS

By May 2013, Kevin Durant had spent 17,595 minutes on court in NBA games, the equivalent of 294 hours, or just over 12 full days.

TAKING TO THE STREETS

One of the reasons that Kevin Durant is so popular is his willingness to visit town and city parks and public basketball courts in order to show off his skills and inspire others.

Before the start of the 2011-12 season, NBA action was put on hold for six months after an argument between club owners and the league over money. During that period, known as the NBA lockout, many players played abroad. Kevin decided to stay mainly at home, and traveled around the country playing games of "streetball," a form of outdoor basketball,

STAR STATS

In his appearance at Rucker Park in 2011, Kevin Durant scored 66 points in the game, just six points short of the venue's all-time record.

and informal pick-up games. During the lockout, Kevin even turned up at Harlem's famous Rucker Park, playing on the same court where many basketball legends have played. The event was part of the Entertainers Basketball Classic series of games.

During the summer of 2011, at the height of the NBA lockout, Kevin headed to China for a six-day tour to promote the sport. He made appearances in four different Chinese cities, participating in coaching sessions and playing streetball with local youngsters. He received a great reception wherever he went, and was a big hit with Chinese basketball fans.

In a surprise appearance during the 2011 NBA lockout, Kevin arrived unannounced at Oklahoma State University to play in a flag football game.

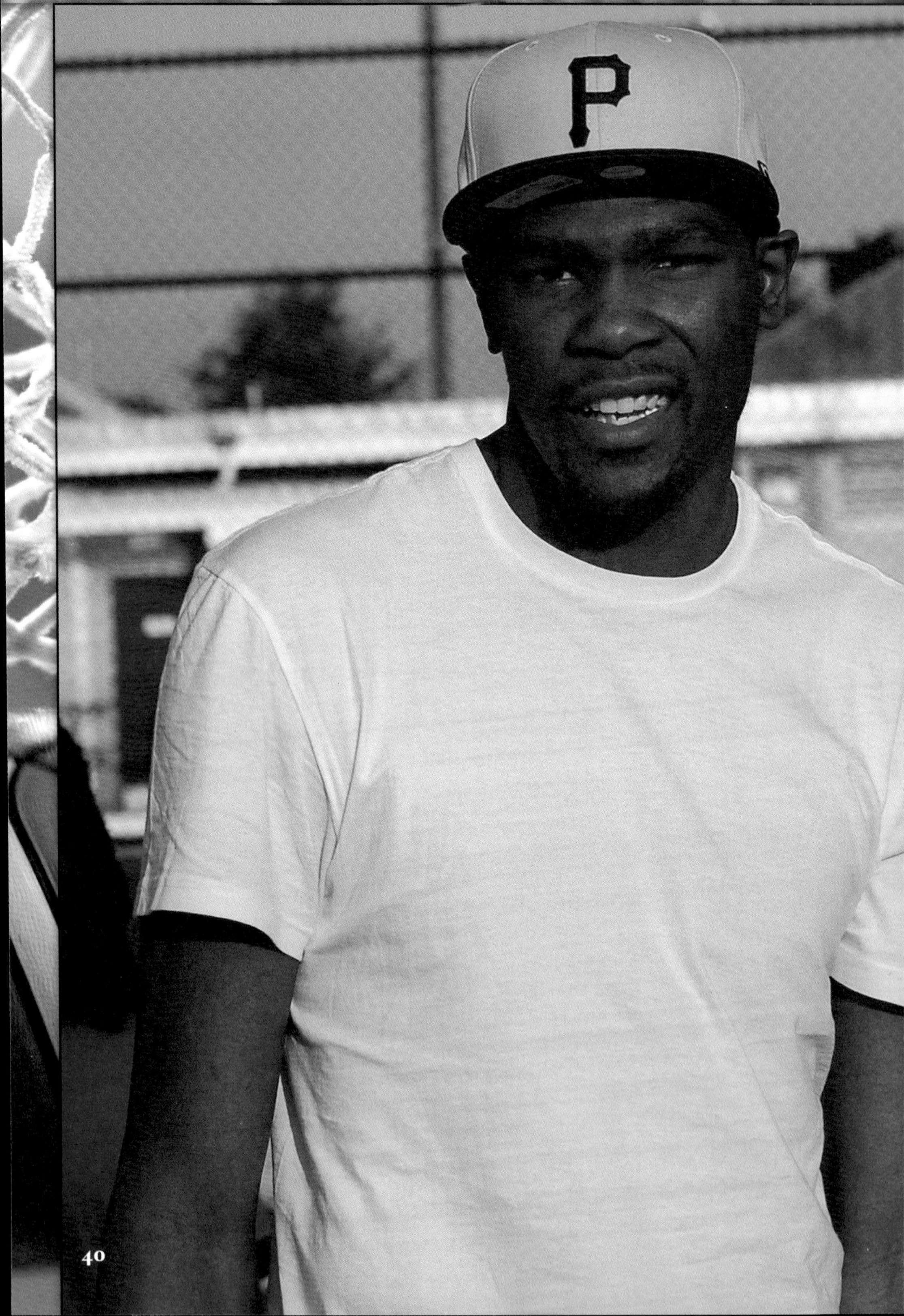

RAGS TO RICHES

Part of Kevin's appeal is his life story, specifically his rise from one of Washington, D.C.'s poorest neighborhoods to global sports superstar.

Kevin's childhood was not easy. He stood out from many of his peers because of his passion for his sport and his disinterest in local gang activities, which included unhealthy pastimes such as drinking alcohol and taking illegal drugs. As a result, kids in the area where Kevin grew up bullied the budding basketball star. Kevin often escaped a beating only by running as fast as he could to the local recreation center. There, the determined youngster spent hours working on his basketball skills, with the aim of one day making it as a professional player.

The example set by Kevin's mom, Wanda, is equally inspiring. Kevin's mother often worked long night shifts in order to provide for her family, showing her sons that commitment can overcome adversity.

Kevin's story sets the example to young people growing up in difficult circumstances that, with determination and the support of your family, you can succeed and break free of a disadvantaged background.

COMMUNITY GREAT

Kevin is unusual in that, unlike many leading professional athletes, he rarely attracts criticism from the press. There is little to be said about Kevin that is negative. The basketball star is honest, hardworking, generous, humble, and always strives to make the best of his talents as a basketball player.

These attributes alone would make Kevin a respected athlete, but he is also greatly admired as a person. This is in no small part due to his willingness to donate his time and money to charity and work for good causes.

Kevin has raised and donated hundreds of thousands of dollars to fund after-school programs, reading programs for children, and charities that work to support single-parent families. Kevin is notable for his generous actions and high-profile position as one of the country's finest sporting role models. This inspirational athlete's contributions to the community have made a difference in thousands of lives.

Since playing his first NBA game in 2007, Kevin (seen dunking during a 2011 summer-league game in Washington, D.C.) has worked just as hard off the court for the charities he supports as he has on the court.

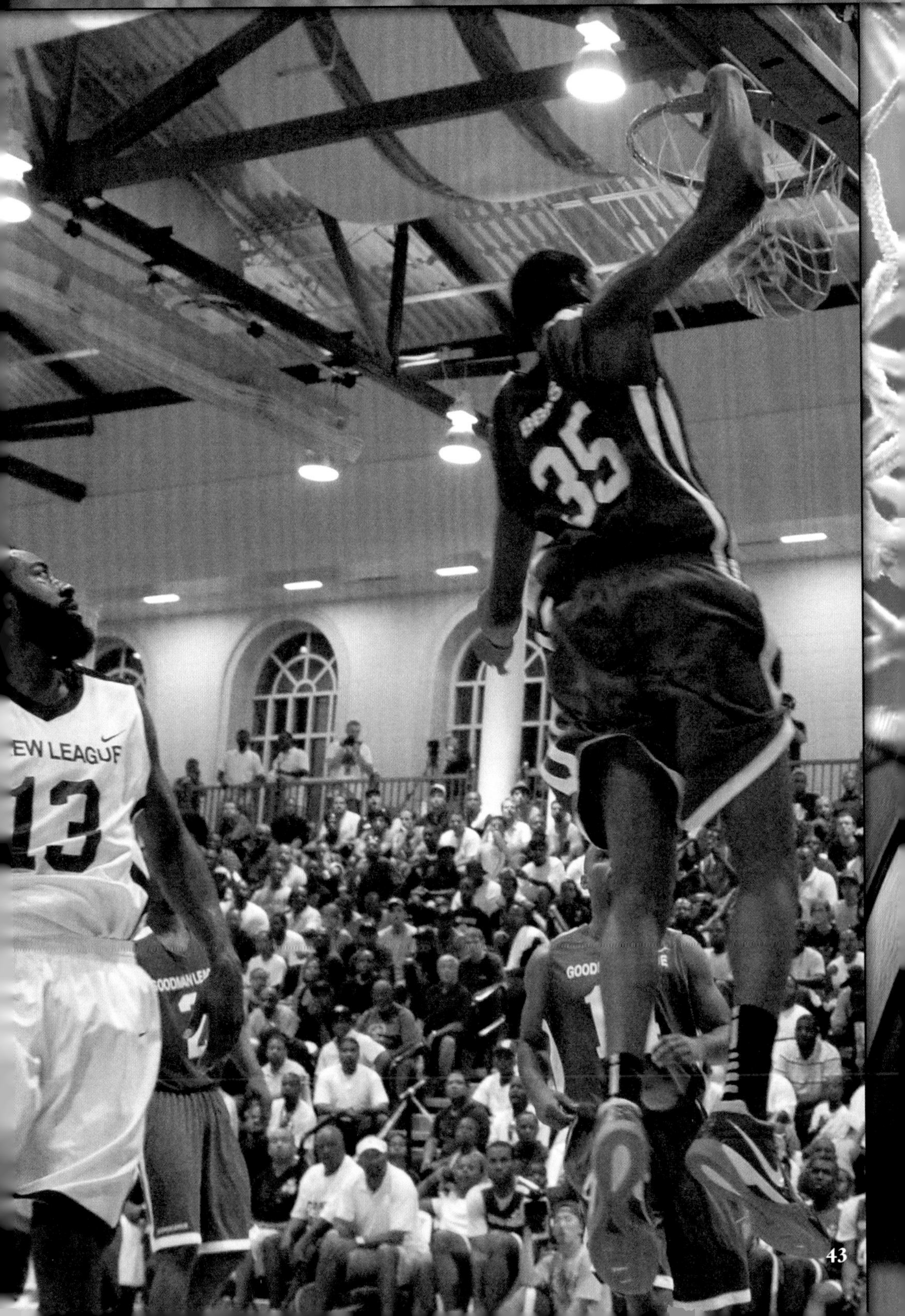
35
13

2000: Kevin and the PG Jaguars win the Youth Basketball of America Tournament.

2006: The star studies at the University of Texas. In his freshman year, he starts all 35 games for the University of Texas Longhorns, the college's basketball team.

2007: In February, Kevin becomes only the second freshman college player to be invited to train with Team USA.

2007: Kevin is named the 2007 Naismith College Player of the Year and 2006–07 Big 12 Player of the Year.

2007: The star makes himself eligible for the 2007 NBA Draft, and signs with the Seattle Supersonics.

2007: In December, Kevin hosts the first "Kevin's Christmas" event for underprivileged kids in Seattle.

2008: He wins the NBA Rookie of the Year award for the 2007–08 season. His Seattle Supersonics team moves to Oklahoma to become the Oklahoma City Thunder.

2010: Kevin signs a five-year $86 million contract extension with the Thunder.

2010: Kevin wins gold as part of Team USA at the FIBA World Championship in Turkey.

2011: During the NBA lockout, Kevin devotes his time to traveling around the U.S. and China, holding coaching clinics and playing streetball games with youngsters.

2012: Kevin scores 36 points in the 2012 NBA All-Star Game, a performance that earns him the Most Valuable Player award.

2012: Kevin becomes one of the stars of the London 2012 Olympics as Team USA wins basketball gold.

2012: He sets up the Kevin Durant Family Foundation.

2013: In February, Kevin scores 52 points in a 117–114 overtime win against the Dallas Mavericks, a career-high scoring record for him.

OTHER SPORTS LEGENDS IN THEIR COMMUNITIES

Jeff Gordon
The leading National Association for Stock Car Auto Racing (NASCAR) driver works tirelessly to raise money for cancer charities.

Robert Griffin III
The pro football player began volunteering for a number of charities while in college.

Mia Hamm
The leading soccer player's Mia Hamm Foundation raises money for families of children suffering from rare diseases.

Tony Hawk
The skateboarding legend's charity, The Tony Hawk Foundation, has provided more than $3.4 million to build 400 skate parks around the United States.

Derek Jeter
The New York Yankees shortstop started his Turn 2 Foundation to support youth programs across the United States.

Magic Johnson
The NBA legend founded the Magic Johnson Foundation in 1991, to fund a range of educational projects. Today, 250,000 young Americans benefit from its funded projects every year.

Peyton and Eli Manning
The record-breaking Super Bowl MVP brothers support many causes through fundraising, including the work of the PeyBack Foundation, the charity set up by Peyton Manning.

Kurt Warner
The former Super Bowl MVP's First Things First Foundation improves the lives of impoverished children.

Venus and Serena Williams
The record-breaking tennis players devote huge amounts of time to charity. They are also fearless campaigners for equal rights for women.

approachable Friendly and easy to talk to.

Big 12 A sports organization set up by 12 leading colleges in the south, midwest, and west of the United States.

campaigners People who work to achieve a specific goal, such as raising money for charity.

community A group of people in one particular area.

devoted Completely committed to something or someone.

disadvantaged To have few opportunities in life.

donates Gives something to a charity or organization.

engage To connect with.

focus A goal or an objective.

fundraising The process of raising money for charity.

initiatives Programs or projects.

inspire To do something that encourages others to follow your example.

literacy The ability to read and write.

memorabilia Objects from a particular time and place that help people to remember that time in history.

NBA The National Basketball Association, the organization that runs professional basketball in the United States.

pick-up games Quick games of basketball, often on a public court, featuring only invited players.

playoff A winner-takes all game. In the playoffs, only the winners progress to play the next match. For the losers, their season is over.

priorities Most important tasks or objectives.

retire To withdraw from use.

role model A person whose good behavior and attitude inspires others.

rookie A player in their first year as a professional athlete.

scholarship Money won by a student in order to study.

sponsors People who give money to an athlete or team in order to be associated with their success.

streetball A variation on basketball, played with slightly different rules, without umpires on a public court, usually outdoors.

underprivileged To have few advantages in life.

Books

Bankston, John. *Kevin Durant* (Blue Banner Biography).
Hockessin, DE: Mitchell Lane Publishers, 2013.

Doeden, Matt. *Kevin Durant: Basketball Superstar* (Superstar
Athletes). North Mankato, MN: Capstone Press, 2012.

Gitlin, Marty. *Kevin Durant: NBA Superstar* (Playmakers).
Minneapolis, MN: Sportszone, 2012.

Sandler, Michael. *Kevin Durant* (Basketball Heroes Making a
Difference). New York, NY: Bearport Publishing, 2012.

Savage, Jeff. *Kevin Durant* (Amazing Athletes). Minneapolis,
MN: Lerner Classroom, 2011.

Web sites

Due to the changing nature of Internet links, Rosen
Publishing has developed an online list of Websites related to
the subject of this book. This site is updated regularly. Please
use this link to access the list:

http://www.rosenlinks.com/mad/duran